Writer/creator

I am a nurse student, who
is passionate about psychology. I want
to share my knowledge and
realizations hoping they could help
someone. 🤍

"Butterfly hug" is a small guide for self compassion, anxiety
management and emotion regulation.

In my next release "Butterfly effect" I will process
neuropsychology and clinical psychology on more deeper level.

With 🤍 : Elina

Human and neuropsychology

Human is psychophysical being- mind and body are straightly connected to eachother. Brains are conductor of that finetuned entirety and very complex system itself- there is approximately 86 milliard neurons, which process and transmit information from senses through impulses. Neurons can associate in numeral different ways into neural net which causes each humans brains to be unique.

Neurotransmitters are unions which regulates impulses between neurons. In this book we will deal with neurotransmitters such as endorphine, oxytocine, serotonine, cortisol and adrenaline.

Nervous system is splitted in autonomic and somatic nervous system.
Autonomic nervous systems actions are involuntary and it is splitted in sympathetic and parasympathetic system. Somatic nervous system is voluntary.

When you start to understand neuropsychology and regulate your own neurotransmitters actions you can reach your full potential.

Neurochemistry

Sympathetic
nervous system-
activation

Parasympathetic
nervous system-
relaxation+
winding down

Vagus nerve-
activates
parasympathetic
nervous system

Autonomic nervous
system-
involuntary actions

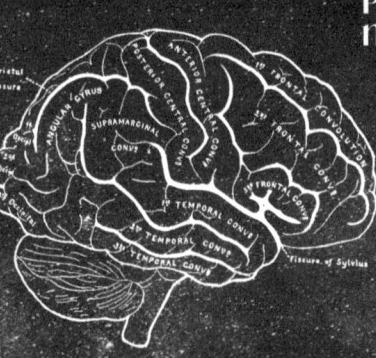

Somatic
nervous system-
voluntary actions

Cortisol-
stress

Oxytocin-
feeling of love
and trust
+ stress relief

Adrenaline-
fight or flight
mode

Serotonine-
feeling happiness
it affects mood +
quality of sleep

Dopamine-
motivation,
communication
+ happiness

Endorphine-
pleasure +
pain relief

Ships don't sink because of the water around them; ships sink because of the water that gets in them. Don't let what's happening around you get inside you and weigh you down.

-Anonymous

Anxiety

Anxiety is natural and primitive reaction to stress- it has been important part of human kind survival. When humans were still on the level of hunter-gatherer, there were dangers in the surroundings constantly- anxiousness helped humans to notice the danger and survive. These days there is not constant danger anymore, but the feeling of anxiousness is still there. Anxiety come out as psychological and somatic symptoms- psychological sypmtoms include restlesness, problems in consentration and circulous thinking. Somatic symptoms include accelerated breathing and pulse, sweating and nausea.

Humans who have high anxiety levels would have been amazing guardians during stone age, but in modern life style anxiety cause more harm than good. It is possible to learn to manage the anxiety so it does not limit your life anymore by using drug-free anxiety management skills.

Anxiety-management in concrete way

❀ Breathing exercises- breath calmly in and out- activates parasympathetic nervous system

❀ Cold shower/ice cubes cold water on the face

❀ Walking + spending time in the nature

❀ Scents like lavender- there is naturally linanool in lavender which activates parasympathetic nervous system

❀ Touch such as butterfly hug- put your arms across your chest and pat yourself calmly

❀ Objectivity towards your thoughts

❀ Focus on what you can affect

❀ Which optimistic thought could decline the negative one

Anxiety management

Anxiety can be regulated by affecting
on following elements:

Optimistic thinking
and objectivity

Physical experiences
induce circle of thoughts
thoughts induce physical
experiences

Activating vagus nerve
parasympathetic
nervous system

Thoughts

Physical
experiences

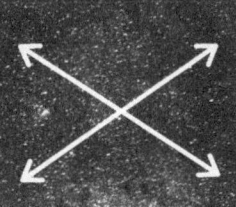

Action

Feelings

Do the opposite than the feeling leading
you to do
when you have self-destructive
thoughts/anxiety is overwhelming,
instead of hurting yourself/ shutting
down do physical exercises/self care

Action, thoughts and physical
expereinces
affect emotions and vice versa induce
positive feelings

Ways to activate vagus nerve

The vagus nerve (lat. nervus vagus) is
the tenth cranial nerve on the neck coming near to the surface +
the main parasympathetic nerve

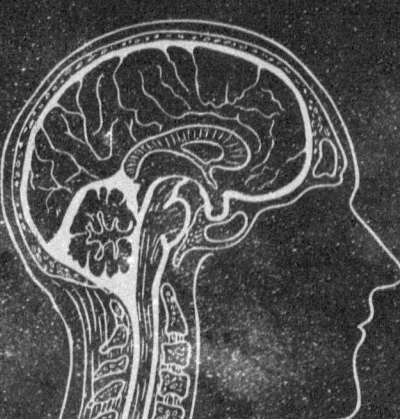

Concious breathing

Exercising

Meditation + gratitude

Reducing caffeine intake

Humming + singing

Nature + forest baths

Laughter

Spending time with loved ones

Gargling water

Using senses- smells, cold water on skin and touch

Fasting, healthy diet+ probiotics

Life will only change when you
become more committed to your
dreams than you are to your
comfort zone

-Billy Cox

Cycle

Cycle is based on the idealogy of dialectical cognitive therapy. Dialectical cognitive therapy is an psychotherapy method created by Marsha Linehan which purpose is to help humans to change their destructive behavioral patterns and teach emotion regulation skills.

Cycle portraits how thoughts, emotions and actions are connected and how you can break the vicious cycle they create by changing their connection.

For example anxiety disorder- human starts to avoid situations that causes anxiety such as going to public places. By doing that anxiety increases- cycle guide human to face distressing situations despite the anxiety and by facing those situations- anxiety eases.

Cycle can be adapted to any intensive feeling- by acting conversely than the negative feeling is leading to- behavioral pattern starts to change.

Cycle

Thoughts

Act different-
when you feel like staying
inside- go outside

Negative thoughts
leads to
negative feelings

Change your
mindset-
do not act by your
emotions

Negatiive feelings
affect wellbeing

Live by caring
about yourself
even when it is
hard

Thoughts, emotions
and action are
connected to
eachother

Action

Feelings

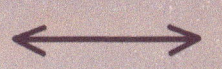

Break the cycle

You are more than your
diagnosis, emotions
and thoughts

Emotion regulation

Observe your thoughts and emotions objectively

Thoughts

Are your thoughts valid?

Be as objective as you can

Use antidote-
Which positive thought could decline a negative one?

Put things in right dimension

Feelings

Let your feelings come and go

Validate your feelings without clinging onto them

This too shall pass

Detach yourself from overwhelming situation to protect your peace

Understand that you can only affect on yourself and your reaction- no one else is resposible about your feelings and you are not responsible for other s reactions.

You can survive from any storm you face

Feelings are visitors—
let them come and go
—Mooji

Self compassion

Self compassion is an ability to face yourself kindly and mercyly even when you fail and there is struggles in your life- using and developing it is important for resilience.

Self compassion

Be a parent for your inner child

See your inner child- how would you talk to child version of you?

Heal your inner child. What were you left without as a child? Give it to yourself.

Identify your inner wounds and treat them.

Validate your feelings and keep your boundaries

Be kind to yourself

Treat yourself the way you treat your loved ones

Speak beautifully to yourself

Take care of your body + mind

Encourage yourself- look at yourself in the mirror and speak supportively to yourself- it is a real psychology hack

Encouraging phrases
🌸 You are enough
🌸 You can survive anything you face
🌸 Nothing external define your value- you are worthy of love and happiness nevertheless

Inner child

When it is hard to face yourself with compassion- take your hand a picture of yourself when you were a child- how would you talk to child version of you?

Remember that behind many destructive behavioral patterns there are wounds of inner child - by treating them, also your behavioral patterns starts to change.

Benefits of crying

Releases happy hormones endorphine and oxytocin, which relief both psychological and physical pain

Helps to process feelings and experiences

Restores emotional balance

Prevent feelings from bottling up

Releases toxins and stress hormones

Activates parasympathetic nervous system

Every time you thought you couldn't move forward you did. Take a moment to appreciate how strong and capable you are.
--Karen Salmansohn

Serotonine

Serotonine is a "happy hormone"- it is important for psychological and physical well being. Serotonine regulate mood and affect numeral physical functions such as body temperature and the regulation of feeling of hunger+ sleep quality.

Serotonine naturally

Healthy diet. which include tryptophan protein such as poultry/tuna/soy. nuts/seeds. spinach+ dark chocolate

Supplements- pure tryptophan. 5-HTP. probiotics

Regular exercise releases endorphine and serotonine

Improving sleep quality

Massage increase blood circulation and decreases cortisol levels

Activating vagus nerve- stress management

Touch releases oxytocin- for example hugging and petting an animal

Gratitude + optimistic thinking

Bright light

Dopamine

Dopamine is a "happy hormone"which
works as a source of motivation and
regulates human s circadian rhythm it has
been important for the evolution as it gives
reward for humans about the actions that
are useful for the evolution.
Dopamine is also responsible for addictions,
whether it was drugs, gaming or social
media humans get addicted to dopamine
and the momentary euforia it gives.

These days humans are exposed to "dopamine peeks" due to the use of mobile device and social media/other stimulants modern life offers- it has a negative effect on the brains "natural" production of dopamine weakens due to the "fake" dopamine and it is harder to focus, get motivated or commit to your ambitions. Dopamine peeks set your dopamine levels so high the levels then crushes down.

The natural and steady production of dopamine can be however strenghten by your own actions.

Dopamine naturally

Reading a book- requires focusing and releases dopamine steadily

Listening music

Projects + studying

Avoiding the use of stimulants caffeine, nicotine and sugar.

Hobbies

Reducing the use of mobile device and social media

Factors that affect also e.g serotonine- healthy lifestyle, regular execising. meditation etc..

Commiting to ambitions- achievements

Going out of your comfort zone to achieve your ambitions

Sleep

Sleeping purifies the brain. cerebrospinal fluid washes the brains and remove harmful metabolic waste. During sleep brains process things that happen during the day and new engrams are developed.
During deep sleep cell damage is repaired and the connections between cells gets stronger especially in the areas which are important for cognitive functions.

Good sleep quality improve both physical and psychological health.

How to improve sleep quality

Sleep hygiene

Optimized environment quiet room, low enough temperature etc

Reducing technology use blue light especially before sleeping

Reduced light at evening

Creating routines + sleep cycle

Magnesium at evening

If you use melatonin, small amount (0.5-1mg) instead of larger amounts is affective and does not mess with natural melatonin production

Lavender oil

Put lavender oil on your wrists before going to sleep it has a calming effect

No caffeine 6 hours before going to sleep

Relaxation techniques

Winding down reading a book, ASMR/calm music, yoga/stretching +conscious breathing

The way you look at the world–
create your reality.

© 2023 Elina Alenius
Kustantaja: BoD – Books on Demand,
Helsinki, Suomi
Valmistaja: BoD – Books on Demand,
Norderstedt, Saksa
ISBN: 978-951-56-8967-2

More material:

David Eagleman's books:
The brain- The story of you+
Livewired

motivation app   psychcentral.com

helpguide.org   Sandi Mann-
-meditations etc   Psychology: A
                                   Complete Introduction

School of life
materials + "The Calm
Workbook"